DATE _____ TIME _____

THEME _____

TECHNIQUES COVERED

WHAT YOU LEARNED

WHAT TO IMPROVE

DATE _____ TIME _____

THEME _____

TECHNIQUES COVERED

WHAT YOU LEARNED

WHAT TO IMPROVE

DATE _____ TIME _____
THEME _____

TECHNIQUES COVERED
WHAT YOU LEARNED
WHAT TO IMPROVE

DATE _____ TIME _____
THEME _____

TECHNIQUES COVERED

WHAT YOU LEARNED

WHAT TO IMPROVE

DATE _____ TIME _____
THEME _____

TECHNIQUES COVERED
WHAT YOU LEARNED
WHAT TO IMPROVE

DATE _____ TIME _____

THEME _____

TECHNIQUES COVERED

WHAT YOU LEARNED

WHAT TO IMPROVE

DATE _____ TIME _____
THEME _____

TECHNIQUES COVERED
WHAT YOU LEARNED
WHAT TO IMPROVE

DATE _____ TIME _____
THEME _____

TECHNIQUES COVERED
WHAT YOU LEARNED
WHAT TO IMPROVE

DATE _____ TIME _____
THEME _____

TECHNIQUES COVERED

WHAT YOU LEARNED

WHAT TO IMPROVE

DATE _____ TIME _____
THEME _____

TECHNIQUES COVERED

WHAT YOU LEARNED

WHAT TO IMPROVE

DATE _____ TIME _____
THEME _____

TECHNIQUES COVERED

WHAT YOU LEARNED

WHAT TO IMPROVE

DATE _____ TIME _____
THEME _____

TECHNIQUES COVERED

WHAT YOU LEARNED

WHAT TO IMPROVE

DATE _____ TIME _____
THEME _____

TECHNIQUES COVERED
WHAT YOU LEARNED
WHAT TO IMPROVE

DATE _____ TIME _____
THEME _____

TECHNIQUES COVERED
WHAT YOU LEARNED
WHAT TO IMPROVE

DATE _____ TIME _____
THEME _____

TECHNIQUES COVERED

WHAT YOU LEARNED

WHAT TO IMPROVE

DATE _____ TIME _____
THEME _____

TECHNIQUES COVERED
WHAT YOU LEARNED
WHAT TO IMPROVE

DATE _____ TIME _____

THEME _____

TECHNIQUES COVERED

WHAT YOU LEARNED

WHAT TO IMPROVE

DATE _____ TIME _____
THEME _____

TECHNIQUES COVERED

WHAT YOU LEARNED

WHAT TO IMPROVE

DATE _____ TIME _____

THEME _____

TECHNIQUES COVERED
WHAT YOU LEARNED
WHAT TO IMPROVE

DATE _____ TIME _____

THEME _____

TECHNIQUES COVERED

WHAT YOU LEARNED

WHAT TO IMPROVE

DATE _____ TIME _____

THEME _____

TECHNIQUES COVERED
WHAT YOU LEARNED
WHAT TO IMPROVE

DATE _____ TIME _____
THEME _____

TECHNIQUES COVERED

WHAT YOU LEARNED

WHAT TO IMPROVE

DATE _____ TIME _____
THEME _____

TECHNIQUES COVERED

WHAT YOU LEARNED

WHAT TO IMPROVE

DATE _____ TIME _____
THEME _____

TECHNIQUES COVERED
WHAT YOU LEARNED
WHAT TO IMPROVE

DATE _____ TIME _____
THEME _____

TECHNIQUES COVERED

WHAT YOU LEARNED

WHAT TO IMPROVE

DATE _____ TIME _____
THEME _____

TECHNIQUES COVERED
WHAT YOU LEARNED
WHAT TO IMPROVE

DATE _____ TIME _____
THEME _____

TECHNIQUES COVERED

WHAT YOU LEARNED

WHAT TO IMPROVE

DATE _____ TIME _____
THEME _____

TECHNIQUES COVERED

WHAT YOU LEARNED

WHAT TO IMPROVE

DATE _____ TIME _____
THEME _____

TECHNIQUES COVERED
WHAT YOU LEARNED
WHAT TO IMPROVE

DATE _____ TIME _____

THEME _____

TECHNIQUES COVERED

WHAT YOU LEARNED

WHAT TO IMPROVE

DATE _____ TIME _____

THEME _____

TECHNIQUES COVERED

WHAT YOU LEARNED

WHAT TO IMPROVE

DATE _____ TIME _____
THEME _____

TECHNIQUES COVERED

WHAT YOU LEARNED

WHAT TO IMPROVE

DATE _____ TIME _____
THEME _____

TECHNIQUES COVERED
WHAT YOU LEARNED
WHAT TO IMPROVE

DATE _____ TIME _____

THEME _____

TECHNIQUES COVERED
WHAT YOU LEARNED
WHAT TO IMPROVE

DATE _____ TIME _____
THEME _____

TECHNIQUES COVERED
WHAT YOU LEARNED
WHAT TO IMPROVE

DATE _____ TIME _____

THEME _____

TECHNIQUES COVERED

WHAT YOU LEARNED

WHAT TO IMPROVE

DATE _____ TIME _____
THEME _____

TECHNIQUES COVERED
WHAT YOU LEARNED
WHAT TO IMPROVE

DATE _____ TIME _____
THEME _____

TECHNIQUES COVERED
WHAT YOU LEARNED
WHAT TO IMPROVE

DATE _____ TIME _____

THEME _____

TECHNIQUES COVERED
WHAT YOU LEARNED
WHAT TO IMPROVE

DATE _____ TIME _____
THEME _____

TECHNIQUES COVERED

WHAT YOU LEARNED

WHAT TO IMPROVE

DATE _____ TIME _____

THEME _____

TECHNIQUES COVERED
WHAT YOU LEARNED
WHAT TO IMPROVE

DATE _____ TIME _____
THEME _____

TECHNIQUES COVERED
WHAT YOU LEARNED
WHAT TO IMPROVE

DATE _____ TIME _____
THEME _____

TECHNIQUES COVERED

WHAT YOU LEARNED

WHAT TO IMPROVE

DATE _____ TIME _____

THEME _____

TECHNIQUES COVERED

WHAT YOU LEARNED

WHAT TO IMPROVE

DATE _____ TIME _____
THEME _____

TECHNIQUES COVERED

WHAT YOU LEARNED

WHAT TO IMPROVE

DATE _____ TIME _____

THEME _____

TECHNIQUES COVERED
WHAT YOU LEARNED
WHAT TO IMPROVE

DATE _____ TIME _____
THEME _____

TECHNIQUES COVERED

WHAT YOU LEARNED

WHAT TO IMPROVE

DATE _____ TIME _____

THEME _____

TECHNIQUES COVERED

WHAT YOU LEARNED

WHAT TO IMPROVE

DATE _____ TIME _____
THEME _____

TECHNIQUES COVERED
WHAT YOU LEARNED
WHAT TO IMPROVE

DATE _____ TIME _____
THEME _____

TECHNIQUES COVERED

WHAT YOU LEARNED

WHAT TO IMPROVE

DATE _____ TIME _____
THEME _____

TECHNIQUES COVERED

WHAT YOU LEARNED

WHAT TO IMPROVE

DATE _____ TIME _____
THEME _____

TECHNIQUES COVERED

WHAT YOU LEARNED

WHAT TO IMPROVE

DATE _____ TIME _____

THEME _____

TECHNIQUES COVERED

WHAT YOU LEARNED

WHAT TO IMPROVE

DATE _____ TIME _____
THEME _____

TECHNIQUES COVERED

WHAT YOU LEARNED

WHAT TO IMPROVE

DATE _____ TIME _____
THEME _____

TECHNIQUES COVERED
WHAT YOU LEARNED
WHAT TO IMPROVE

DATE _____ TIME _____
THEME _____

TECHNIQUES COVERED

WHAT YOU LEARNED

WHAT TO IMPROVE

DATE _____ TIME _____
THEME _____

TECHNIQUES COVERED
WHAT YOU LEARNED
WHAT TO IMPROVE

DATE _____ TIME _____

THEME _____

TECHNIQUES COVERED

WHAT YOU LEARNED

WHAT TO IMPROVE

DATE _____ TIME _____
THEME _____

TECHNIQUES COVERED
WHAT YOU LEARNED
WHAT TO IMPROVE

DATE _____ TIME _____

THEME _____

TECHNIQUES COVERED

WHAT YOU LEARNED

WHAT TO IMPROVE

DATE _____ TIME _____

THEME _____

TECHNIQUES COVERED

WHAT YOU LEARNED

WHAT TO IMPROVE

DATE _____ TIME _____
THEME _____

TECHNIQUES COVERED

WHAT YOU LEARNED

WHAT TO IMPROVE

DATE _____ TIME _____
THEME _____

TECHNIQUES COVERED

WHAT YOU LEARNED

WHAT TO IMPROVE

DATE _____ TIME _____
THEME _____

TECHNIQUES COVERED

WHAT YOU LEARNED

WHAT TO IMPROVE

DATE _____ TIME _____

THEME _____

TECHNIQUES COVERED
WHAT YOU LEARNED
WHAT TO IMPROVE

DATE _____ TIME _____

THEME _____

TECHNIQUES COVERED

WHAT YOU LEARNED

WHAT TO IMPROVE

DATE _____ TIME _____
THEME _____

TECHNIQUES COVERED

WHAT YOU LEARNED

WHAT TO IMPROVE

DATE _____ TIME _____

THEME _____

TECHNIQUES COVERED
WHAT YOU LEARNED
WHAT TO IMPROVE

DATE _____ TIME _____
THEME _____

TECHNIQUES COVERED

WHAT YOU LEARNED

WHAT TO IMPROVE

DATE _____ TIME _____

THEME _____

TECHNIQUES COVERED
WHAT YOU LEARNED
WHAT TO IMPROVE

DATE _____ TIME _____
THEME _____

TECHNIQUES COVERED
WHAT YOU LEARNED
WHAT TO IMPROVE

DATE _____ TIME _____
THEME _____

TECHNIQUES COVERED

WHAT YOU LEARNED

WHAT TO IMPROVE

DATE _____ TIME _____
THEME _____

TECHNIQUES COVERED

WHAT YOU LEARNED

WHAT TO IMPROVE

DATE _____ TIME _____

THEME _____

TECHNIQUES COVERED

WHAT YOU LEARNED

WHAT TO IMPROVE

DATE _____ TIME _____

THEME _____

TECHNIQUES COVERED

WHAT YOU LEARNED

WHAT TO IMPROVE

DATE _____ TIME _____
THEME _____

TECHNIQUES COVERED
WHAT YOU LEARNED
WHAT TO IMPROVE

DATE _____ TIME _____

THEME _____

TECHNIQUES COVERED

WHAT YOU LEARNED

WHAT TO IMPROVE

DATE _____ TIME _____

THEME _____

TECHNIQUES COVERED
WHAT YOU LEARNED
WHAT TO IMPROVE

DATE _____ TIME _____

THEME _____

TECHNIQUES COVERED

WHAT YOU LEARNED

WHAT TO IMPROVE

DATE _____ TIME _____

THEME _____

TECHNIQUES COVERED

WHAT YOU LEARNED

WHAT TO IMPROVE

DATE _____ TIME _____

THEME _____

TECHNIQUES COVERED

WHAT YOU LEARNED

WHAT TO IMPROVE

DATE _____ TIME _____
THEME _____

TECHNIQUES COVERED

WHAT YOU LEARNED

WHAT TO IMPROVE

DATE _____ TIME _____

THEME _____

TECHNIQUES COVERED
WHAT YOU LEARNED
WHAT TO IMPROVE

DATE _____ TIME _____
THEME _____

TECHNIQUES COVERED

WHAT YOU LEARNED

WHAT TO IMPROVE

DATE _____ TIME _____
THEME _____

TECHNIQUES COVERED
WHAT YOU LEARNED
WHAT TO IMPROVE

DATE _____ TIME _____
THEME _____

TECHNIQUES COVERED

WHAT YOU LEARNED

WHAT TO IMPROVE

DATE _____ TIME _____
THEME _____

TECHNIQUES COVERED

WHAT YOU LEARNED

WHAT TO IMPROVE

DATE _____ TIME _____
THEME _____

TECHNIQUES COVERED
WHAT YOU LEARNED
WHAT TO IMPROVE

DATE _____ TIME _____
THEME _____

TECHNIQUES COVERED

WHAT YOU LEARNED

WHAT TO IMPROVE

DATE _____ TIME _____
THEME _____

TECHNIQUES COVERED
WHAT YOU LEARNED
WHAT TO IMPROVE

DATE _____ TIME _____
THEME _____

TECHNIQUES COVERED

WHAT YOU LEARNED

WHAT TO IMPROVE

DATE _____ TIME _____
THEME _____

TECHNIQUES COVERED

WHAT YOU LEARNED

WHAT TO IMPROVE

DATE _____ TIME _____
THEME _____

TECHNIQUES COVERED

WHAT YOU LEARNED

WHAT TO IMPROVE

DATE _____ TIME _____
THEME _____

TECHNIQUES COVERED

WHAT YOU LEARNED

WHAT TO IMPROVE

DATE _____ TIME _____
THEME _____

TECHNIQUES COVERED

WHAT YOU LEARNED

WHAT TO IMPROVE

DATE _____ TIME _____
THEME _____

TECHNIQUES COVERED
WHAT YOU LEARNED
WHAT TO IMPROVE

DATE _____ TIME _____
THEME _____

TECHNIQUES COVERED
WHAT YOU LEARNED
WHAT TO IMPROVE

DATE _____ TIME _____
THEME _____

TECHNIQUES COVERED
WHAT YOU LEARNED
WHAT TO IMPROVE

DATE _____ TIME _____
THEME _____

TECHNIQUES COVERED

WHAT YOU LEARNED

WHAT TO IMPROVE

DATE _____ TIME _____
THEME _____

TECHNIQUES COVERED
WHAT YOU LEARNED
WHAT TO IMPROVE

DATE _____ TIME _____

THEME _____

TECHNIQUES COVERED
WHAT YOU LEARNED
WHAT TO IMPROVE

DATE _____ TIME _____
THEME _____

TECHNIQUES COVERED
WHAT YOU LEARNED
WHAT TO IMPROVE

DATE _____ TIME _____

THEME _____

TECHNIQUES COVERED
WHAT YOU LEARNED
WHAT TO IMPROVE

DATE _____ TIME _____
THEME _____

TECHNIQUES COVERED

WHAT YOU LEARNED

WHAT TO IMPROVE

DATE _____ TIME _____
THEME _____

TECHNIQUES COVERED

WHAT YOU LEARNED

WHAT TO IMPROVE

DATE _____ TIME _____
THEME _____

TECHNIQUES COVERED
WHAT YOU LEARNED
WHAT TO IMPROVE

DATE _____ TIME _____
THEME _____

TECHNIQUES COVERED
WHAT YOU LEARNED
WHAT TO IMPROVE

DATE _____ TIME _____
THEME _____

TECHNIQUES COVERED
WHAT YOU LEARNED
WHAT TO IMPROVE

DATE _____ TIME _____
THEME _____

TECHNIQUES COVERED
WHAT YOU LEARNED
WHAT TO IMPROVE

DATE _____ TIME _____
THEME _____

TECHNIQUES COVERED
WHAT YOU LEARNED
WHAT TO IMPROVE

DATE _____ TIME _____
THEME _____

TECHNIQUES COVERED
WHAT YOU LEARNED
WHAT TO IMPROVE

DATE _____ TIME _____
THEME _____

TECHNIQUES COVERED

WHAT YOU LEARNED

WHAT TO IMPROVE

DATE _____ TIME _____
THEME _____

TECHNIQUES COVERED

WHAT YOU LEARNED

WHAT TO IMPROVE

DATE _____ TIME _____

THEME _____

TECHNIQUES COVERED
WHAT YOU LEARNED
WHAT TO IMPROVE

DATE _____ TIME _____
THEME _____

TECHNIQUES COVERED
WHAT YOU LEARNED
WHAT TO IMPROVE

DATE _____ TIME _____

THEME _____

TECHNIQUES COVERED
WHAT YOU LEARNED
WHAT TO IMPROVE

DATE _____ TIME _____
THEME _____

TECHNIQUES COVERED

WHAT YOU LEARNED

WHAT TO IMPROVE

DATE _____ TIME _____
THEME _____

TECHNIQUES COVERED
WHAT YOU LEARNED
WHAT TO IMPROVE

DATE _____ TIME _____

THEME _____

TECHNIQUES COVERED

WHAT YOU LEARNED

WHAT TO IMPROVE

DATE _____ TIME _____
THEME _____

TECHNIQUES COVERED
WHAT YOU LEARNED
WHAT TO IMPROVE

Printed in Great Britain
by Amazon

64806547R00071